The Easter

The item should be returned or renewed by the last date stamped below.

Dylid dychwelyd neu adnewyddu'r eitem erbyn y dyddiad olaf sydd wedi'i stampio isod.

PILL

_____ _____ _____

_____ _____ _____

_____ _____ _____

_____ _____ _____

_____ _____ _____

_____ _____ _____

_____ _____ _____

_____ _____ _____

_____ _____

To renew visit / Adnewyddwch ar
www.newport.gov.uk/libraries

ry

For Maureen Veronica

Gracious thanks to Mira Avrech, Abraham Rosenthal and the Israel Tourist Board
for their great kindness and generosity in the preparation of this book

OXFORD
UNIVERSITY PRESS

Great Clarendon Street, Oxford OX2 6DP

Oxford University Press is a department of the University of Oxford.
It furthers the University's objective of excellence in research, scholarship,
and education by publishing worldwide in

Oxford   New York

Auckland   Cape Town   Dar es Salaam   Hong Kong   Karachi
Kuala Lumpur   Madrid   Melbourne   Mexico City   Nairobi
New Delhi   Shanghai   Taipei   Toronto

With offices in
Argentina   Austria   Brazil   Chile   Czech Republic   France   Greece
Guatemala   Hungary   Italy   Japan   Poland   Portugal   Singapore
South Korea   Switzerland   Thailand   Turkey   Ukraine   Vietnam

Oxford is a registered trade mark of Oxford University Press
in the UK and in certain other countries

First published 1993
First published in paperback 1994
Reissued in paperback 1999 and 2008
This new edition first published in paperback 2021

British Library Cataloguing in Publication Data
Data available

ISBN 978-0-19-277852-9 (paperback)

1 3 5 7 9 10 8 6 4 2

Printed in China

Brian Wildsmith
The Easter Story

OXFORD
UNIVERSITY PRESS

Once, a long time ago, a little donkey was brought to Jesus.
The little donkey had never been ridden before, but Jesus spoke gently
to him, and soon he stopped being afraid.

Jesus climbed on to donkey's back, and they set off for Jerusalem.

As they drew near to the city, there were great crowds of people standing by the road. The little donkey was amazed to see so many people.

Some had spread their clothes along the road. Branches cut down from
the palm trees were spread there too, all for him to walk on.

'Hosanna!' the people shouted. 'Hosanna! It's the man who comes from God.'

By the time they reached Jerusalem, the crowds were filled with excitement. Some people were asking, 'Who's that, sitting on the back of the donkey?' Others replied, 'It is the prophet Jesus, from Nazareth in Galilee.'

The little donkey lifted his head proudly as they entered the city.

The little donkey carried Jesus through the streets
until they stopped in front of the temple. Jesus went inside and saw
that it was full of people busy buying and selling.

He drove them all out, shouting, 'My house is supposed to be a house of prayer, not a den of thieves!'

For the rest of that week, the donkey stayed with Jesus in the city.
On Thursday night they walked through the streets to a small house,
and Jesus went in to have supper with his friends. Through the window
the little donkey saw Jesus breaking the bread.

'Take and eat this,' said Jesus. 'It is my body.' And the donkey watched as
Jesus lifted up a cup of wine. 'Take and drink this,' Jesus said. 'It is my blood.'

At last they came to the house of Caiaphas, the High Priest.
The donkey heard Caiaphas ask Jesus, 'Are you the Son of God?'
    'I am,' Jesus replied.

Then the High Priest said, 'You have heard these terrible words.
What do you say?'
    'He deserves to die,' they all cried.
    The crowd left Caiaphas' house, and took Jesus to Pilate, the Roman Governor.

The little donkey watched as Jesus stood in front of Pilate and
a huge crowd of people.

'Are you the King of the Jews?' asked Pilate.

'Those are your words,' said Jesus.

The priests then accused Jesus of many things. 'Have you no answer to make?' said Pilate. But Jesus did not reply.

'What shall I do with him?' asked Pilate.

'Crucify him,' they all shouted.

'Take him and crucify him, then,' said Pilate. 'I wash my hands of him.'

So the soldiers took Jesus away. They put a crown made of thorns
on his head, and made fun of him. 'Hail, King of the Jews,' they said.
They gave him a huge cross of wood and forced him to carry it.
'If only I could help him,' thought the donkey sadly.
But a man came out of the crowd and helped Jesus
to carry his cross.

The little donkey followed as they led Jesus to a hill
outside the city.

There they crucified him between two thieves.

Late that night, a rich man named Joseph asked Pilate for the body of Jesus. He wrapped the body in a clean linen sheet, but it was too heavy to carry.

Joseph placed the body of Jesus on the donkey's back, and the little donkey carried it to a new tomb which had been cut out of the rock. Joseph laid the body inside and rolled a huge stone in front of the entrance.

Early on Sunday, two of Jesus' friends came to the tomb.
But when they got there, they found that the stone had been
rolled away and the body of Jesus was gone.

The donkey saw two angels where Jesus' body had been.
'He is not here,' the angels said. 'He is alive again.'

The women left the tomb and the donkey followed until they came to a
garden. A man was standing there. The women thought that he was the
gardener, but the little donkey knew it was Jesus.

The women were frightened, but Jesus said to them, 'Don't be afraid.
Run and tell my friends to go up to Galilee, and they will see me there.'

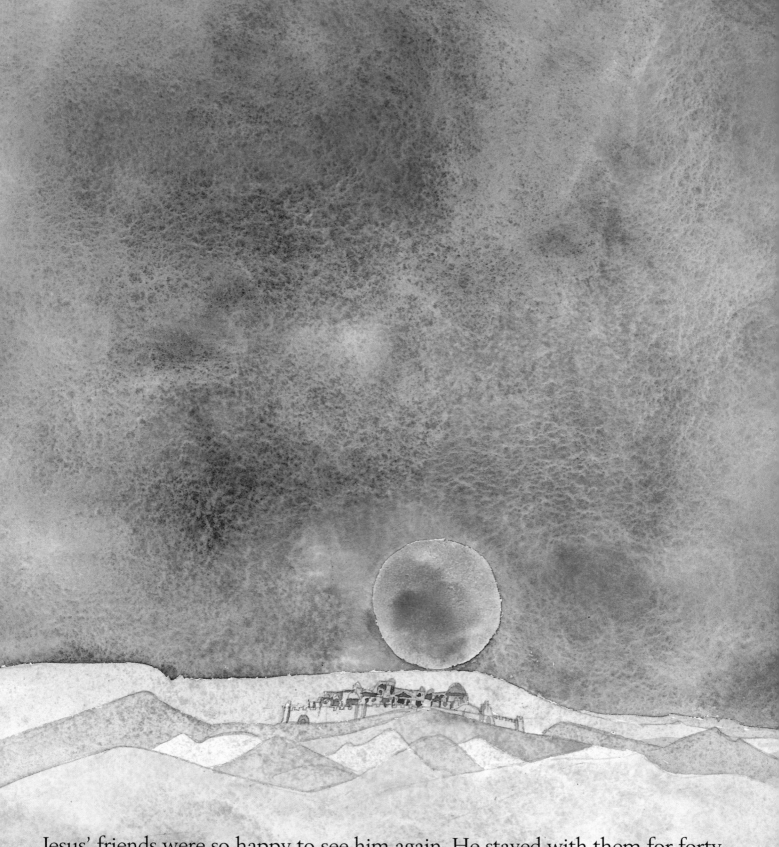

Jesus' friends were so happy to see him again. He stayed with them for forty days, teaching them about the Kingdom of God. But Jesus knew that it was near the time for him to leave this earth.

As the sun rose one morning, he went up to his father in Heaven.

The next day, one of Jesus' friends took the little donkey back to his home.
And the little donkey stayed there for the rest of his life, remembering the
kind and good man he had carried on his back to Jerusalem.